T0113544

DR. OVELL'S TESTIMONY
BOOK 1

OVELL BARBER

authorHOUSE®

AuthorHouse™
1663 Liberty Drive
Bloomington, IN 47403
www.authorhouse.com
Phone: 833-262-8899

Published by AuthorHouse 08/09/2021

ISBN: 978-1-6655-3367-6 (sc)
ISBN: 978-1-6655-3366-9 (e)

Library of Congress Control Number: 2021915530

Print information available on the last page.

This book is printed on acid-free paper.

I dedicate this book to my late mother and grandmother, "Ella May" and "Hattie May". And, to all the Christians in the world. Thus, Christianity is a very special religion.

My name is "Ovell T. Barber", and I have been locked up in the Virginia prison system for (30) years! I got locked up in Norfolk, VA back in (1988), and it was three seperate charges in which the Norfolk Circuit Court convicted and sentenced me to; Robbery - 3 years, Murder - 90 years, and failure to appear - 1 year. This gave me a total sentence of (94) years!

During these (30) years of incarceration, I decided that now was the time to share my TESTIMONY with the world, with hope and prayer that someone will find and receive JESUS CHRIST, MY LORD AND SAVIOR!!!

For GOD and his son JESUS are the reason why I am who I am today and until he call me home. They kept me on this earth to share my TESTIMONY. And, if you start reading this book and you're not a Christian, by the time you finish reading this book you may want to become a Christian. And, by the way, every thing that is written in this book is the truth, by way of actual facts and events.

I was the sixth child born into a very loving God Fearing family. I came into this world on "September 5, 1967". I was born in Depaul Hospital in Norfolk, VA. My family and I was living in a housing project called "Tidewater Park". My memory as a little child go all the way back to three to four years old.

My sister Peaches and I was very close. She used to walk me to school every morning, "Tidewater Park Elementary". She was the oldest, and I was the youngest between six kids, until my younger brother Cornell was born, by way of his dad "Big Cornell", and my mom. My dad left my mom when my mom was pregnant with me.

My grandmother "Hattie May" helped my mom raise seven of her kids! My grand mother had a very strong will, but that will and strength came by way of her belief in God and his son Jesus!!!

Every Sunday morning, as far back as I can remember, my mother "Mrs. Ella May" made sure that we went to church, to give prays and thanks to a God that I didn't know any thing about. However, my oldest sisters didn't have to go to church, Nadine (Peaches); Vera (Dimples); and Leterell, (Pebbles). But, they would help us (the younger siblings) to get ready for church. And, my mom used to say that I was going to be a preacher. I guess that she would say that because I used to mimic them old Baptist Preachers real good. But, as a child, you mimic what you see.

My mother never set down and actually read the Bible to her kids, nor did my grandmother. And, when my mom did read the Bible to her kids, she only read the "Book of Revelation". They would verbally tell us about JESUS, because they heard the story all of their lives, and they truly knew him in their own way. My mom and grandmother only had a fourth grade education. But, my mom could read a little. And, I didn't know this about them until they passed away, because they were so smart, that they hid it well.

I now know and understand that my mom and grandmother did the best that they could do to teach their kid's about God and his son Jesus, regardless of their way of teaching it, and the fear tactics that they used to teach about God and his son Jesus. Because, they both knew that one day that they would both leave us, and they both knew the very best that they could ever leave us with was God and his son Jesus.

When I was a baby living in "Tidewater Park", one of the bad things that happened to me was "crawling in the oven" trying to get to my grandmother's cornbread. I was told by my sister Nadine, aka, (Peaches), "that I got burned really bad. Both of my legs and arms had to be rapped like casts for a very long time, and both of my hands." She said, "my grandmother didn't see me crawling into the oven, but she heard me crying." I didn't have no memory of this as I got older. However, my sister (Peaches) wanted me to know every thing that happened to me when I was a baby.

She also told me that, "after I had healed from being burned up, that my sister Vera, aka, (Dimples), was keeping me one day, and dropped me right on my head in the living room!" Peaches said that, "my mom beat Dimples so bad for that, because she thought that I was going to die or have brain damage". I don't have no memory of this either, but Peaches made sure that she told me about what had happened to me.

In addition to being burned and dropped on my head as a baby, when I was only four years old, I do remember this. One day me and my brother James, aka, (Popa), was in our bed room playing, but decided to hang our young bodies half way out our bed room window, which is the second floor of the project apartment in "Tidewater Park". So, as we hung our little bodies half way out the bed room window, side by side, my brother James decided to cuss out the neighbors next door, whom was also looking out of their bed room window. But, they were teenagers, and they didn't care about nothing, they were young thugs for real!!!

James learned how to cuss at an early age by listening to the adults. I could hardly talk, so I wasn't doing no cursing. As he started cursing the neighbors out, they started looking around in their bed room for something to throw at my brother James, aka, (Popa). We both saw this, and started wiggeling back inside the window at the same time. Popa was stronger than me, so he got back inside the bed room first. Right after he got in, the big rock was coming, and I couldn't duck it!!! It hit me right in the center of my for head and nocked me out! My little body was hanging halfway out of the window, and halfway in the bed room. Popa thought that I was dead, he started calling for my mom, I could hear him in the distance, because I was still conscious somewhat.

Blood was running from the center of my for head, and I just knew that my mom was going to take me to the hospital, to the doctor or something. But, instead, her and my Godmother, "Ms. Arlen", only rapped a rag around my head, and put a sliced potato on the wound. They then gave me instructions to lie there, and not to move. Nothing was done to my neighbors, because they were the nephews of "Big Cornell", my mom's boy friend, (my little brother's dad).

Although I was having it rough as a child. I was very loved, and I always felt protected. For some strange reason, my mom felt the need for me to go and get Baptized after this event.

I got Baptized by my Godmother's brother. He was a preacher, that was also a hustler. Supposedly, he gave his life to God. However, his church was an old movie house that was converted to a storefront church in a neighborhood called "Park Place" in Norfolk, Va. And, to my surprise, it was a lot of people there that night. It was a lot of people standing in the line to get Baptized, and I was in the back of the line. However, I was the first one called up front to get Baptized.

It was done in a big tin barrel. As my head was being dipped in the water, all I could think about was, "why was I called first to be Baptized?" Saying to myself also, "surely others should go before me, for they are more worthy than me". But, the preacher, my Godmother's brother, thought that I should be first to get Baptized.

As a little boy, not even being able to read the Bible, "I didn't have a clue what a Baptism was". However, I did feel that it would give me some kind of protection. Even more protection than I was already feeling. And, I truly felt that this was the beginning of something good, but I didn't know what.

My family moved to another housing project after that. It was called, "Robert's Park". My brother James and I had gotten a little older, and a little wiser. I was either seven or eight years old, and he was nine or ten. One day my brother and I was comparing the life lines in both of our hands, and he started joking the life lines in my right hand, saying, "your main line stop, and don't match your other hand, and you got a spot in your hand".

My brother was only acting as a child would act. We used to joke on one another all the time. But, this time my sister "Peaches" was observing us, and she didn't like what she was seeing, nor hearing. She called me and told me to come to her. When I got to her, she told me to sit down, and that she had something to tell me.

My sister "Peaches" called me to her, and told me to look into my hands. She told me that I crawled into the oven when I was a baby, and that both of my arms, hands, and legs got burnt real bad. She told me how my arms, hands, and legs had to be rapped in cast like material. She then said, "that is why your hands have a burnt mark on them, but your right hand shows it more".

My sister had me looking all over my body, because I would never have known, or guessed that I was a burnt victim when I was a baby. And, she also told me how my sister "Dimples" dropped me on my head when I was baby.

As I looked over my body, I discovered something that "Peaches" did not tell me about. My left leg, "on my shinbone got it the worse!" I could see that they drafted skin over it. But, as a young boy not knowing what had happened to me, I played real rough, and I kept hitting that leg, in that spot. And, gradually, the skin draft started coming off a little bit. The scar was ugly, but beautiful to me, because I survived that oven!!!

When we moved to "Robert's Park" housing project, this was the first time that I heard my grandmother speak about evil people and witches. She was from "North Carolina", so, she have seen some things, and heard some things. And, she made sure that she told me and my brother James who house not to play around. And, all the houses that she pointed out, was occupied by real old women (her age) that she did not want us playing around their house. Well, as I got older, I found out that those women were working (roots), and somehow my grandmother knew this without even talking to anybody about it.

But, my brother and I was determined to explore the entire neighborhood, and beyond. We was older now. However, my brother heeded my grandmother's wisdom better than I did. When I wanted to go and play in certain people yard, my brother would stop me, and stop himself. As the oldest boy, it was his job to look out for me. But, we played real rough and dangerous.

My brother James and I was playing in the house

one day on the top of the stairs. We was taking turns swinging one another on a wooden pole hanging above the stairs. I don't know why the housing authority had that pole there, but we used it to swing on. Until one day, my brother James decided to push me real hard as I was swinging on this wooden pole. And, he pushed me with all of his might!!! I went flying down the stairs, feet first. But, when my body landed, "the back of my head hit the corner of the bottom step".

My grandmother heard the noise and came running to the steps, "just to see her grandbaby lying there in a puddle of blood! This was the first time that I heard my grandmother scream. She was screaming for my mom, but my mom wasn't at home. Ironically, my mom had just pulled up in her car, being in no rush to come inside. My grandmother made my brother James go and get her.

When my came inside, and looked at me, she didn't panic right away, because she thought that i just fell down the stairs My grandmother was crying hysterically, and told her no! He got pushed down the stairs, and his head is bleeding! When they lifted me, "they saw that I had to be taken to the hospital.

My skull got cracked, and my mom stood over me the entire time that surgery was being done, and I was wide awoke during surgery. They stopped the bleeding, numbed me up real good, then they put some type of mesh over the hole that was in my skull. My mom told me that I could have died.

I felt that something was protecting me, but I did not know what it was. My mom still made us go to church, and by this time in my life, I could read the Bible, but I didn't fully understand it. I was around eight years old.

After this tragedy, "I went to my first family reunion in (North Carolina). I saw for the first time in my life, "people riding horses in the street". This was the real south!!!

However, what was also real was the fear that I saw in my grandmother, when her sisters look her to an old grave cite in "North Carolina" during our family reunion. She took me with her, and she held my hand real tight. It was a lot of woods surrounding this small grave cite. And, when the elders gathered around this particular grave cite, the bushes and trees started shaking, and the wind started blowing harder, and my grandmother pulled me without warning, and started a very fast walk back to the car. She took off without warning any one! It was something that my grandmother knew about, but she also knew about Jesus!!! When my grandmother and I got into the car, "she locked the doors and started praying".

When we got back home from the family reunion. I started experiencing something that was very strange to me, and when it first started happening to me, I was ashamed to tell any one, because I didn't want no one to look at me as if I was crazy, or telling a lie.

I would get tired during the day time, and take a nap on the sofa in our living room. There were a lot of people living in this project apartment, but they would always seem to be gone around this time of day (noon). As I would sit on that sofa wide awoke, "I would become paralyzed, and could not move nothing!!!" Then, I felt myself falling in this black hole. I just kept falling deeper, and deeper, and deeper, and deeper!

Then, an anxiety came over me, talking to me as well. Telling me that, "if someone come through that front door, that I would be able to move. And, if someone was to come and touch me, that I would be able to move". If this did not happen, "I knew, and felt that I was going to die right there on that sofa". But, to my surprise, my brother James would come through the door every time, and whatever it was that was holding me, it would release me, and I would be gasping for air

This evil took place with me every time that I would sit on this sofa when no one was around. It was like something was trying to take my soul. First it would paralyze me, having me not being able to talk, move, or any thing. Then, it would slowly start taking my breath away! But, like I said, "I didn't tell any one because I was ashamed". However, it got so bad with me, until one day I broke down and told my brother James. And, the only reason that I told him was, he walked through the door one day and I started gasping for air.

My brother James asked me what was wrong, and I broke down and told him. But, to my surprise, he didn't look at me as if I was lying, nor did he look at me as if I was crazy. My brother looked at me and said, "guess what?" "The exact same thing be happening to me when I be sitting on that sofa in the living room and no one is around". This gave me some comfort, but not a lot. Because, neither one of us knew what it was, and for some reason we never told our mom.

Approximately one year after telling my brother James what was happening to me, and him telling me what was happening to him, "my mom moved our entire family to my grandmother's home, in a neighborhood called Campostella".

My brother James didn't know that, "whatever evil spirit that that was trying to capture our soul, 'it made me believe in God more, and his son Jesus', and I was so young with all of these spiritual feelings inside of me, but I just couldn't understand it, nor explain it. But, I kept going to church, because I was always raised to believe in God and his son Jesus!!! And, something inside of me always told me that God and his son Jesus was the right way. Because of this, I was always different from my peers, and people in generation when it come to material wealth. I always knew that money was needed, but I just wasn't caught up on worldly things like a lot of people.

I can remember the first day when my family moved into my grandmother's home. It was a very exciting time, something to call our own!!! No more housing project!!! My grandmother's home was made of brick, and it initially had two bedrooms, one bathroom, a kitchen, and an attic. But, before we moved into this home, my mom had three more bedrooms added on to this home, and another bathroom.

Also, I was glad to be leaving behind that sofa, and that end row apartment. Because I knew that evil lived in that apartment, and, my brother James did to. However, when we moved into my grandmothers home on the first day, we started cleaning up the entire property. But, when we made our way to the attic, we found something in that attic that really made my mom and my grandmother very upset!!!

My mom was called up into the attic by my older sister's, because they made their way up there first. Always seeking to get their hands on my grandmother's belongings. However, this time, not only did they find a lot of my grandmother's belongings, but they also found jars, upon jars, upon jars of roots! It was revealed that, "whomever the man was that my grandmother was renting her home to, was working roots! But, in my little mind, it was so many jars of roots, that he had to be a "root doctor!!!"

Little kids coming up in the south would learn

things about (roots), just by listening to the older people talk.

My mom called all of her kids into that attic, and told us not to touch any of those jars, and nothing else in that attic until she cleaned it up. My mom went and got her Bible, some gloves, garbage bags, and some type of herb to burn. She started reading the Lord's Prayer, and burning that herb, at the same time throwing all of those jars of roots into her big green trash bags. I stood there and watched her, and she did not let us help, nor touch any of those jars.

Those jars to me, "looked like they had green slime in most of them. But, some of them had green dry stuff in them. Some of them jars may have been a different color than green, but all of those jars was very wicked looking! And, some was bigger than others, but none of them was smaller than a regular size peanut butter jar".

It was a lot of stuff up there in that attic that us kids wanted, but, after my mom discovered all of those jars of roots, she wanted to throw away every thing that was in that attic! But, the main thing that we wanted her to keep was the professional "pool table" that was up there in that attic. But, my mom had her way, and cleaned that attic out!!! And, she just didn't go up in the attic and pray that day, "she called a minister and had him to pray up in the attic, and to pray over the entire home.

I never thought that I would hear the speach again that my grandmother gave to my brother James and I when we first moved to "Robert's Park", ("don't go play in people yard, etc.") But, this time, it wasn't just James and I whom she gave her speach to. She gave it to all of her grand kid's this time, and it went something like this; "witches live in this neighborhood, do not deal with these people in this neighborhood".

I started attending "Diggs Park Elementary" school. I loved living in Campostella. I thought that it was a good neighborhood. Campostella is seperated by three different sections. "Campostella Heights"; Campostella Fields"; and Campostella. My family and I lived in Campostella.

My church that I claimed was "First Baptist Church" on "Canoga Street". For some strange reason, that's the church that I gravatated to. I didn't attend like I was suppose to, but that was the church that not only did I claim, but my family to.

I learned early on that people in Campostella was very private people. They didn't want strange poor kids like myself playing with their kids. I learned later on that prominent people lived in my neighborhood. Business owners, school teachers, doctors, lawyers, etc. I didn't know that they looked at me as if I was some kind of disease, but they did. But, the funny thing was, "it was many of those same black families who looked at me like I was a disease, who used to borrow money from my grandmother, and would beg her for a ride to the hospital when one of their family members would get sick.

It was a lot of danger in Campostella, but I guess that I was too blind to see all of the danger back then. Campostella was surrounded by a lot of water, and it have plenty of shipyards. But, it also had railroad tracks leading to a neighborhood called "Berkly".

I used to hang out with the roughest guys that I could find. One of them was "T". But, I started hanging around "T" because he lived in the part of Campostella where a beautiful young girl used to live. And, I just had to visit "T", with hopes that I could see her playing out side in front of her house. Her name is "Serena Carter". I didn't know what love was back then, but I do know that I felt something very special inside of me each time that I saw her. We were very young, attending "Diggs Park Elementary", "Tarralton Elementary", and then "Campostella Junior High".

As we got a little older, "T" stabbed one of our friends in his neck with a broken bottle in front of "Diggs Park Rec Center". I wasn't at the rec center that day, but I did see our friend some days later. It was true, "T" did it. He couldn't fight, he was just wild, and didn't care. When "T" stabbed our friend, that should have been my warning sign to stopp hanging around "T". But, "I just had to go around "T's" house to see if I could see "Serena". Back then, you just didn't go to other people side of the neighborhood without somebody with you from that part of that neighborhood.

Our friend only received stitches in his neck, but any one could tell that he wasn't the same after that. He started drinking real bad after that incident, and later in the years died from being a junkie and an alcoholic.

One day while hanging out with "T" down "Berkly", the neighborhood annexed to "Campostella" with a lot of railroad tracks, in which "was the day that ended my football career", in which I was very good at playing".

As we walked the railroad tracks in "Berkly", "T", and "D", "D" being from Diggs Park, and myself, looking for something mischievous to get into. As we walked into the cross roads of the railroad tracks in "Berkly", we saw the track rail, in which was designed to guide the trains to keep going in the right direction. If you take the safety from off of it, you could swing it all the way around just like a merry go round. Well, we did just that. We would take turns swinging one another. And, we was mindful that we was surrounded by railroad tracks, and that a train could come at any time.

When it was my turn to sit on this contraption, "T" had the bright idea to convience "D" to help him to push me real fast so that I couldn't jump off of this contraption without hurting myself. So, as I was surrounded by train rocks, and railroad tracks, I couldn't jump without hurting myself. But, I knew that I had to jump before a train started coming. If I didn't, "I was a dead man because they couldn't stopp the momentum of the contraption, it was too big! However, it stopped itself with a Sutton stop! Because the safety lock came down, "and, I went flying backwards head first, landing head first right into a railroad track!!!"

They thought that I was dead. They started to leave me until they saw that I started to move a little bit.

Blood was running from my head as if it was coming from a water fountain!!! I could not move, I could not pick myself up. All I could do was beg them for help. I could see in their eyes that they wanted to leave me, but something stopped them. As they lifted my body from that railroad track, they looked at my head and told me that I was hurt real bad! The blood was running so hard, that it made them even more scared as they started walking me down the tracks to the road looking for help.

As we made it to the main road, they flagged a car down to take me to Campostella. It was an older man who stopped to give us a ride. And, he wasn't going to give us a ride until we saw the blood running from my head.

He dropped me off at my mother's house in Campostella. "T" and "D" took off running home after they helped me from out of the man's car. I told him thanks, and he said, "no problem", and took off.

I guess that it was so much blood, that none of them thought that I was going to make it.

I made my way inside of the house, bleeding like crazy. My mom wasn't home. My brother "James" and my sister "Tonya" was at home. When they saw the blood, "they automatic asked me who did this to me." For some strange reasons I didn't respond. They got mad with me because I would not tell them. They took me in the bathroom and started shaving the hair from around the hole in my skull. Popa thought that he was a doctor or something, and Tonya did to. But then common sense set it, and they both realized that I had to go to the hospital.

What was strange about this incident, as I sat there bleeding real bad, I felt protected, but I didn't know what it was. A calm came over my body, as I sat in that house waiting on my mom to come home. Tonya and James didn't want to call the ambulance, because it cost too much money! So, they would rather I die before calling the ambulance for their dying brother.

When my mom finally arrived, she got mad at me

and didn't want to take me to the hospital. See, she worked at " Norfolk General Hospital", and now she must go back to work to take me to the emergency room. The blood was still running from my head real fast, even after all of this time had went by. God was with me. My own family didn't care if I would have died.

Just like the last time when I lost a piece of my skull, "the doctor left me wide awoke, shot needles in my head to numb me up, and then covered the hole with some kind of mesh." But, this time I almost broke my neck. I could not move my head to the right, nor to the left. When doctor started telling my mom about my injury, and told her that I was lucky to be alive, she was no longer mad that she had to take me to the hospital. As a matter of fact she started to cry. I left that hospital with staples in my head, and wearing a neck brace.

When I awoke that morning after coming home from the hospital, "I knew that I could not play football any more". My coach got mad with me when I told him that I couldn't play any more. I knew that if I got hit in the head one more time, (playing football or any thing with a head on collision), "that

I was going to have brain damage or something". My coach knew about the injury, but he didn't care.

During this sad time in my life, "I started slowing down, and looking deeper at the things that was going on around me." I should've been dead, but here I was still alive! If a train was coming at the time my head was on that railroad track, "my entire head would have got cut off".

Also, when I got home from the hospital that night, "my mom made sure that I slept in the bed with her that night". The doctor told her not to let me go to sleep. And, that when I did doze off," he told her to watch me real careful, because its a good chance that I could go into a coma." I heard my mother praying that night.

Because of this injury I had to stay out of school for a little while. My mom would make me walk down the street to the fish market. For some reason, my mom loved eating fish! And, something else was revealed to me about my mom during this time of my absence from school. "My mom read her Bible each and every day". This was something that I didn't know about my mom. She may have had her flaws, "but I had a praying mother, and a "God Fearing Mother!!!"

As I would walk to the fish market, "it was always this one house on my block that would raise the hairs on the back of my neck when I would walk pass it." This house was an evil house, "I could feel it". Sometimes when I would walk pass this house, "it felt like the house was looking at me'. This was a crazy feeling,but "I" was already familiar with feeling the presence of evil spirits,and "I" was also familiar with evil spirits trying to take my soul;when i used to sit on that sofa; when my family and i lived in "Roberts Park" ,In the last row apartment.

However, this evil house that made me feel eerie, did not deter me from speaking to this beautiful young lady that was sitting on a porch two houses away, in which she was related to the family who owned the "evil house." At the time I did not know it, but, it was her great grand mother who owned the "evil house". The pretty girl, her name was "Patriece".

In the beginning when I first spoke to her, she acted as if she did not want to speak to me. In my mind, I had to have her because she was so beautiful! But, also in my mind, I knew that I would be going against what my grandmother told me and the rest of my siblings; thus, "do not mess with them people who live down the street." I said to my self, "grandma is wrong about her, she don't even know her."

So, I continued to persue Patriece, and one day she invited me inside of her house. That was a beautiful house to me, with all the comfort a person could want. When I entered into the house I thought that we was going to sit in her living room. That was not the case. She lead me straight to the back of the house to her bed room, where we made love right then and there for the first time.

We became boyfriend and girlfriend. I guess we were a young couple. She loved me and I loved her. The love was very real, no doubt about that. But, I needed better money and more money. I went to Job Corps, but, I didn't like the trade that I took up. I really needed more time to learn, but Job Corps is only two years.

As Patriece and I grew more and more, and loved one another more and more, I felt that God was going to bless me with finding a better job than what I had, in which was a "part time auto mechanic assistant." I knew that her family was a well to do family on the street that we lived on, and, that I had to do something to make some good money, or else, they would not want her to be with me. I could feel that her family was just about money, and not of God, but at the time, I just wanted Patriece.

My next job was at "NorShipCo". I was only eighteen years old working full time at one of the largest shipyards in the world. And, we would also work at the "Norfolk Naval Base". In which is the largest "Naval Base" in the world. So, I was doing okay for myself, because I was eighteen with no kids, and no responsibilities. And, I wasn't on drugs.

It was a guy working in my department that used to work roots, and I kept my distance from him because of this. He was a cool guy, but I didn't deal with him. He also owned a food truck and knew the marshal arts real good. I would always sit in front of my locker in the locker room on lunch break. I would sit there until it was time to go back to work, not dealing with no one unless I had business with them.

However, sometimes this lady name "Ann" would come get me to get each lunch with her, because she didn't want to eat alone. And, she knew me. This was Patriece in-law. Also, "Ann" was also the first cousin to the guy who worked roots and owned the food truck and knew the marshal arts real good. They were first cousins, but I didn't know this.

Patriece and I are doing good, and one day in her own way she asked me to get married to her. But, to be honest, "I never gave marriage thought", but I loved her. She didn't ask me no more after that. Later she became pregnant with my child. Right around this time her great uncle came home from prison, and his dad and mom whom were still living when he came home gave him that "haunted house." His name is "GU".

"GU" had mad issues, but he always seem to have plenty of cocaine! In which a lot of females wanted to be around him when he came home from prison. He spent (21) years in prison for killing a North Carolina State Trooper. And, the word was, "his sister and others went to North Carolina to pay a root doctor to get Patriece great uncle (GU) out of prison. And, "I know this to be true".

Patriece would share all of her family secrets with me. Not only did we both love one another, but she was my friend. And, she started telling me about the people in her family that was working roots.

Not only was her great uncle (GU) having cocaine smoking parties in that "haunted house", but him and his girlfriend was also working roots in that already "haunted house!!!" I guess that one could call it voodoo as well.

As time went on in Patriece and I relationship, our love for one another got deeper. She trusted me more and more with telling me about her family secrets, and, she convinced her aunt (unbeknownst to me) to introduce me to their "family ouija board."

At this time I had been living with Patriece and her grandmother for about two years. However, what was about to be revealed to me, completely shocked me about Patriece, "my girl friend, best friend, and pregnant baby mama". Yes, she was all of that to me. But, what her family was teaching her, had taught her, was very shocking to me.

One day as I came back home, I walked into the house as I normally did, and as I entered into the den, "Patriece and her aunt was sitting there with a ouija board between the two of them." As I entered the room, both of them smiled with a surprise on their face as if I caught them doing something wrong, but happy to see me because, "this was the day (so they thought) that they were going to introduce me to their family 'ouija board'."

Patriece called me to her, because I had stopped right in my tracks as I came through the den's door, and saw what I saw. They were actually playing it, and asking it questions. But, apparently, it wasn't responding to them. As I walked over to Patriece, she started telling me how she was glad that I came home because she wanted me to play the "ouija board" with them.

She wasn't asking me, she was actually telling me the instructions to this evil, and letting me know that I was going to do it with her, because it's suppose to be played between a man and a woman whom was in a relationship with each other.

She grabbed my hand for me to sit down infront of her, where her aunt was sitting. She then resumed telling me how we would utilize this evil. She told me what the dial was, how we was to place our fingers/hands on the dial and ask it questions, etc.

She then placed both of her fingers/hands on the dial, and she told me to do the same and we would proceed to ask this evil thing questions. I was blindly following her voice, but as my hands/fingers were about to touch this evil, something in me pulled my hands/fingers back.

I stood up quickly, and said no! I then told her that I was raised not to deal with this thing or anything like it! I started walking out the room. Patriece and her aunt commence to call me all kind of names. Names like: you're scared (mf),you're a punk etc.

I responded as I kept walking, "I don't care what y'all call me, I don't deal with that stuff, and I never will!" I walked out of the house, down the street, and around the block with a clouded head. I could not believe that Patriece was into this "ouija board" thing so deep, and, I didn't even know this about her, when I thought that I knew all it was to know. How mistaken was I.

I took a long walk that day. She was actually coaching me how to play her family's "ouija board", and, was playing it with her aunt before I entered the den, all the while pregnant with my son. I felt so bad! But, what was I to do? I was dumb, deaf, and blind to so many things. However, I always felt that I was protected.

After living with her and her grandmother for two years in that house, it was just now being revealed to me that they was living with a "ouija board" in that house. Now I was beginning to understand why certain noises could be heard when it was just her and I in the house and, the lights would sometime blink off and on.

And, unbeknownst to me, it was deeper than her family's "ouija board", "they were also working roots. Although it was mentioned earlier in this book about her grandmother helping her brother (GU) getting out of prison via, a root doctor in North Carolina, I did not know that her entire family was into the "ouija board" and working roots until, "after two years of living with Patriece and her grandmother.

Sometimes Patriece would cut my hair, and when she would finish I would volunteer to clean up my hair, "she would never let me". But, what seemed strange to me was, "she was so adamant about not letting me clean up my own hair.

When her grandmother would fix or cook big meals, they would never let me come into the kitchen to fix my own plate. Patriece grandmother would always call her to the side, and tell her to go in the kitchen to fix my food for me. It would always seem strange to me, but, I was dumb, deaf, and blind.

Patriece and I really lived in that house by our selves. Her grandmother would come and go, because she found a boyfriend whom had his own house. Patriece's grand dad had built that house from the ground up. And, I believe he died in that house. However, I believe that Patriece's grandmother new boy friend knew her grand dad, because both of them was into construction work in the Norfolk, VA area. And, this is why he didn't want to come to that house - because he didn't want to disrespect his friend. Yes, his friend.

However, the house was haunted. And, I do believe that it was a combination of the roots that they was working, the grand dad passing away in that house, and that evil ouija board.

After things had calmed down from when I had walked out the house, and refused to play that ouija board, I thought that all of that was behind us. But, that was not the case. One day as we was cleaning up the house, it was revealed to me by Patriece where they kept their family's ouija board. They kept that evil thing behind their big floor model TV in the den.

I was amazed that she (Patriece) kept these evil things from me for two whole years. However, things started taking place so wickedly, that it kind of compelled her to let me in on her family's evil secrets. And, the main one being the family's ouija board.

One day Patriece and I decided to chill in the den, and watch a movie on the big floor model color TV. The TV had cable. We didn't have to go to the movies. So, as we set down on the thick plush carpet in front of that big pretty floor model color TV, it took no more than five minutes, and we heard a rattling noise.

Patriece and I looked at each other. We both knew what it was. It got louder and louder within seconds. It sounded as if, "Whatever her and her aunt was trying to call up, or dial up on that ouija board had come!" It sounded as if it was trying to get from out of the box that the ouija board was in. I looked at her for the second time, and without saying a word to her, "I got straight up and started walking out the door!" She jumped up as fast as she could and started walking right behind me. To my surprise, she was very afraid. But, I could not understand why.

How can someone work roots and be afraid of it? Well, I didn't understand it, but I witnessed it that night. The lights started blinking off and on, and, I knew that whatever it was that they was calling up, had showed up!!!

I don't believe that we stayed there that night, I never saw Patriece scared of any thing. I never saw her afraid of any thing. But, this night, I saw all the fear come out of her. She could not hide it if she tried.

She knew what her and her aunt had been doing. However, the grandmother was coaching them on how to work the roots and play the ouija board. I had no knowledge of calling evil spirits up, or working roots. All I ever knew about when it came to spirits was the "Holy Spirit"," and, that Holy Spirit was God! And, I knew that God gave His son Jesus so that use would be saved from our sins, and, forgiven of our sins.

Although all of these unnatural things was going on in her grandmother's house and her uncle's house. ("GU"), I was still looking for a job, and I needed one bad! Patriece was approximately three months from giving birth to our child. After the "ouija board" incident, I went to see Patriece a few days later. It was early in the morning and she was home alone. She acted as if the "ouija board" incident never took place.

As I greeted her with, "hey, what's up?" She didn't

respond, she just kept walking around the hose cleaning up. Then, catching me off guard, she came walking to me grabbing me on my arm and said, "you got to get out, you don't have no money or a job! And, we have a baby on the way!" She walked me to the door and put me out the house.

This was my first time ever seeing her so angry with me, "and it made me feel terrible in the inside". I didn't want to let her down, and I didn't want to let my child down. So, as I walked away from her grandmother's house, "all that I could think of is, ('how can I get some money right now'), for my family".

When I got to "Wilson Road" I saw the store owner pull up to his store, then he got out of his car with a hand full of money. Then he grabbed a real big wallet to put all of the cash in. It was a bank wallet. Then he made his way to the store to open it up.

I saw an opportunity to get some money for my family. I never robbed any body in my life, now I'm about to Robb a man that will kill me, because his reputation was to shoot and kill. This man also owned another store across town, and he owned a club in the neighborhood "Berkly". No one ever robbed this man and got away! But, I was desperate, "I had a baby on the way".

I waited five to ten minutes after the store owner opened the store, I walked inside the store and walked straight behind the counter and robbed him. I didn't actually Robb the store, I took the bank bill fold from off of his side, where just a few minutes ago I saw that that's where he had put all of the money. He tried to grab under the counter for his gun, and that's when I grabbed him and put him in the head lock from behind. That's when I told him, "I don't want to hurt you, I just want the money".

As he tried to buck, I gently put him on his back and ran out the door as fast as I could. I got to the end of the block something told me to turn around. When I turned around to look back I saw the store owner aiming to shoot. But, it was too late. I was too far away, and I was turning the corner as he was aiming to shoot. I guess that five years of playing running back helped me out, so I thought.

I made my way to a friend house in "Campostella Fields". When I got inside and emptied out the bank wallet, "all that was in it was (old checks) that he had cashed for people, it was no money in that wallet what so ever!!! I was mad, real mad. He had took all of the money out of the wallet as soon as he had got into the store, and put the checks inside of the bank wallet.

I was shortly informed by two childhood friends, that knew where I must have went to after they heard that I was the one who had robbed the store, "that (MB), another childhood friend was telling the police that it was me who had robbed the store based on the description that the store owner gave".

I waited for the police to come. It was no need for me to run. I felt that I didn't take no money, and I didn't hurt no one. Most of all, "I'm going to give everything back to him". Well, it didn't quite work out that way. The police did come, and I gave everything back as I was turning myself in. However, the store owner lied and said that I took ($50.00) dollars from him. Although that statement wasn't in the original police report, "somebody told him to say it, and it stuck". I didn't know nothing about the law, so I didn't fight it.

Patriece was real hurt!!! She had no idea that I was going to do something like that. Well, "I didn't either". All I knew at the time is that, "I had to get some money from my family!" She had just kicked me from out of the house, and I was in panick mode.

Some how, Patriece convinced her grandmother to get me out of jail on bond. I got out of jail, and I went to live with my sister "Peaches" in a neighborhood called "Park Place".

I secured a job on "21st Street" in Norfolk, VA working for "Dumar Warehouse". Patriece and I was getting along good, but now I was facing a robbery charge, and she was a few months from having our baby.

My son came into the world on (June, 1st), and he was my pride and joy!!! I never loved a human being on this earth more than him. I didn't want people touching him, keeping him, playing with him or any thing!!! This was my son, and I was a proud young dad!!! His mom and I was getting along well, and all of a Sutton she started to change on me.

I didn't have much money, but I gave all that I could. I had to pay my sister for staying at her house, and I had to give Patriece money. Basically, "I had no money left for myself". My sister would feed me, and buy me clothing from time to time. Other than that, "I had nothing".

I knew that I had to live the right way. "I was not going to Robb no one, I was not going to sell drugs, I was not going to do wrong no matter what!" I had to raise and take care of my son, "my pride and joy!!!"

After Patriece gave birth to my son, she started dealing with a guy that had just moved accross the street from her uncle's house, (GU), which was the "haunted house". At this time I was living by the under pass going towards "Tidewater Park" in a rooming house by "Norfolk State University". I didn't know that she was cheating, "I was the last one to know".

One day when I called her checking on my son, "she broke down and told me every thing". I was very hurt. But what made me hurt even more, "is when she told me that she had had sex with this guy in the room where my son was at".

I cried for days. The pain was devastating. However, I had to move on. But, she had one of my checks from the warehouse where I used to work at. She went to pick up this check for me when I went to jail for property damage. No charges was issued against me.

One of my childhood friends gave me a ride to her

house. Before we got to her house, "I told him that he had to go to the door and ask her to give him my check for me." I told him what had happened, and that I was leaving, "on my way out of town!" I didn't know where I was going, "but go I must!!!" She didn't give him the check. She brung the check to the car herself. She came to my side of the car, but I had my window rolled up. I couldn't even look at her, "I just wanted to leave".

She told me to roll the window down. She said that if I didn't that she wasn't going to give me my check. So, I did. She then asked me, "where are you going?" I responded, "I'm leaving, I'm just leaving". Before I knew it, "she handed me my son through the window that was rolled down, and then she handed me my check." Then she said, "wherever you're going, take him with you. And, when you come back, come to my uncle's house because that's where I'll be." The uncle was (GU), and the house was the "haunted house".

When I got back to her uncle's house with my son, I gave her uncle's girlfriend my son and I left. Patriece wasn't there. She left to go give her friend a ride home. When she got back and found out that I had left, and what direction I had went in, she came after me.

I was accross the street from "Diggs Park Elementary" when she cought up with me, "on my way out of town!!!" She cought up with me and asked me not to leave. We both just stood there and cried. Some how my mom had heard about I was accross from "Diggs Park Elementary", and she pulled up with her car and told me to get in. I got into her car, and Patriece turned around and went back home, me and my mom left and pulled up and parked in front of "First Baptist Church".

I told my mom that I was okay, and that I didn't need a ride. My mind was on my son, and I really didn't want to leave him. So, I told my mom that I was okay, and I left. I went wondering around all night, thinking, "should I leave, or should I stay?" I knew that I had to be at court for the robbery charge, but, in my mind I just wanted to leave town. But, something said do the right thing.

The next morning I asked Patriece to walk down to my mother's house with me, (which is on the same street), with my son, "because my mom was going to give me a ride to court, and I wanted to spend this time with him". She came, but she started arguing when we got half way, in which was her uncle's house, the "haunted house".

We went inside of her uncle's house, and her uncle's girlfriend was there. I sat on the couch, Patriece was standing between the kitchen and the living room. And the girlfriend had the baby. Patriece started arguing some more, about how she didn't want to take the baby down to my mother's house, and I was just sitting on the couch listening to her.

The girlfriend went out side with the baby. And just as soon as the girlfriend went out side with the baby, "an evil spirit entered into me from that ('haunted house'), and just like a zombie, I had no control over my thoughts or my body." I got up and went into the kitchen where Patriece was at, I grabbed a nife and I stabbed her in the neck three time. Right after that, I left out the back door and walked down the street to my mom's house. I went into the kitchen, grabbed a nife and stabbed myself in the neck. After the first thrust, "whatever evil spirit had entered into me had left from out of me.

I was in my mother's house on the floor dying. Someone had called the police and the ambulance.

As I was lying on the floor in my mother's bedroom, I could hear someone running through the house. I had to get up and see who it was, I could barely stand up, I was almost dead. As I stood up, just getting ready to take a step, a police came running in the room with his gun drawn.

He called the ambulance. It was a white woman and a black man. They cut off all my clothing with some scissors. I was losing blood at a very fast rate. I could tell by the look on their face that I was not going to make it. I went out, and came back momentarily. They was talking to me, trying to keep me woke. All I could remember before I went out for the second time was a detective. He was running beside the rolling bed trying to ask me some questions, as the ambulance crew was running me into the hospital on the rolling bed. They told him to stop trying to ask me questions because I was dying, and they was trying to save my life. I went out again for the third time. I died, so I thought. I don't really know.

I could only see and hear. I was being kept alive by a breathing machine. The Chinese lady was the doctor who operated on me. When I opened my eyes, she started telling me who she was and what it was that she did to me. I did not understand a word that this lady was saying. And, as far as my eyes could see, "I was in some kind of medical ward or room, where every body was barely hanging on to life, and it seemed like all of us was just brung back to life".

I had a box on my chest that was full of blood, and I was breathing through something that looked like a straw that was connected to a machine. They said that blood went into my lungs and that they had to pump it out, and I couldn't breathe on my own.

I tried to snatch that thing out and just die! But, they had me in some kind of hand cuffs, as if I was going somewhere! I just came back from death, and was about to die again. I could barely move! And, I could barely breathe! I wanted the suffering to end.

As I looked into that mirror, "I was seeing staples all the way around the front of my neck!" I felt so bad! I was looking like a monster!!! All that I could ask God was, "why me Lord?" "Why was I still living?" I always believed in God and his son Jesus, and I would never put no God before him. So, I really didn't understand why this terrible ordeal was happening to me, or taking place in my life.

I couldn't talk because of the neck injury. And,

my energy level was on zero! I was so weak until they had to wait for a few days before they started giving me therapy. However, the Police and the Deputy Sheriff would never close my door to my hospital room. They would keep it open at all times, even when they was changing shifts.

My mom and my sister came to visit me, but they was not allowed to come into my room. It was my sister Nadine with her, aka, (Dimples). They stood at the door, and my mom broke down crying. She looked at me and said, "I wish that you was dead!" I was not expecting for her to say that, and her statement put pain on top of plain, when I thought that I could feel no more pain than what I was already feeling. Because, unbeknownst to her, "I really wanted to be dead so that the pain could go away!!!"

I couldn't speak, and I could barely move my hands, "but I managed to move my hands just enough to motion to them to leave as tears streamed down my face". I wondered, "why would my mom say such a thing like that to me?" Some years later "Dimples" answered that question for me. She said, "moma said that because she didn't want to see you suffer". I understood.

Right in front of my hospital room, just a little to the left, it was an elevator. I could literally see people getting off and on this elevator. However, it was an old lady walking with a cane that I didn't see get off of this elevator, but, she appeared and was walking with slow motion straight to my hospital room. I'm thinking that the Norfolk Police was going to tell her that she had to stop, that she couldn't come into my room like they told my mom and sister. But, they did not say one word, and she walked right in.

She came in the room and stood by the bed. One of the Police Officers pulled up a chair so that she could sit down. This lady had to be in her (90's) going on (100!) After she sat down, she started to talk. She said, "baby I came here today to visit my friends. I know who you are. Every thing is going to be alright. You just keep right on believing in God". She then said, "I know that you can't talk, but that's okay. You just keep on believing in God and every thing is going to be alright". This was so spiritual to me, very spiritual.

Shortly thereafter, the "Norfolk Police" came to the hospital to take me to jail. With two holes in my neck, and wear like no one should be, "I was on my way to face the unknown" (jail/prison). All together, I spent (31 yrs & 6 months) incarcerated in the Virginia prison system.

I went into the jail and prison with plenty of sorrow and pain. I wanted to undo what I did, "although it wasn't me - but an evil whom entered into me." All that I had was God and His son Jesus. All that I ever had was God and His son Jesus.

I kept the faith! I never turned to no other religion while incarcerated, I never would leave nor sway from my Christian belief in Jesus Christ as my Lord and Saviour.

I went into the jail and prison not being able to read and write that good. I didn't have a "high school diploma," nor did I have a "GED." I was lied on by the "Commonwealth Attorney" concerning the homicide, and, my "court appointed attorney" aided and assisted the commonwealth attorney to convict and sentence me to a 90 years prison sentence.

However, I made parole after serving 31 years and 6 months incarcerated in the VA Prison system. Although I was issued a "second degree murder indictment," and, it was never changed to a "first degree murder indictment," I was convicted and sentenced to (first degree murder) illegally!!!

But, Glory be to God and His Son Jesus! He made sure that His Spirit was always covering me, and the Blood of Jesus!

I went in without a (GED) and plenty of sorrow and pain! However, I came out with a (PHD) and always placing a capital letter in the beginning of His holy Name!!!

TO BE CONTINUED
BOOK-2
"Dr. Ovell's Testimony"

Printed in the United States
by Baker & Taylor Publisher Services